The Fragrance of
WORSHIP

*Bringing your worship to a
deeper and higher level*

By
ROBERT SOVERALL

BIOGRAPHY

A s a child growing up in Brooklyn, New York, I was heavily impacted by music; nothing else moved me so deeply. As I grew, the stories of the Bible also began to make a strong impression on my life and my thinking. I was in church every week and, as I matured, I became very much involved in the "program" of my church. After giving my life to the Lord again, at the age of 16, I believed I was headed for the height of spiritual "achievement". By the time I was 30, I was an Elder in my church, a teacher, an accomplished pianist with a Bachelor of Science and a Master's Degree in Performance, had a beautiful wife, a nice car, and a good hold of the message of the Bible...or so I thought.

My personal worship, despite all these achievements, was stifled, if not retarded. I knew there was more. I'd seen the power of GOD's word in action; I'd felt the power of GOD's Spirit in the music I was creating and endorsing. However, my personal worship was controlled and sometimes even clinical. As a consequence, when I entered into the more serious trials of young adulthood (navigating a new marriage, dealing with a disappointing job), I discovered that church programs, theological debates or a good song could not help me cope with or conquer my problems. However, when I began to travel in music ministry, a whole new world opened to me.

I began to see that GOD didn't want me to just learn about Him or sing about Him, but that He wanted me to **know** Him.

My concepts of the church, of music, the Scriptures and of worship changed drastically over these years. It was during this time of learning that GOD inspired the words you are about to read.

My only hope is that when you've finished reading, you too will begin a journey that will draw you away from mere knowledge and religion, while leading you into intimacy, submission and oneness with GOD. And I pray that our quest for deeper worship will *be met only by a deeper understanding of the living GOD and of what He's calling each of us all to be.*

GOD be with you,
GOD be praised,

Bobby

ACKNOWLEDGEMENTS

Thank you Patricia, Judah, and Rebekah for being three great reasons to do what I do... and to come home after doing it.

Thank you Louis, Jerry, Neda and Gillian for faithfully planting the seeds God gave you into my heart and life. The event that gave birth to this work was blessed because you all were a part of it. And now, because of you, many more will be blessed. May blessings come back to all of you, and to those you call dear.

Thank you, Val, for helping me take the first steps in putting it all together! You are a gift.

Thank you, Alvin Slaughter!

Being around and learning from you has taken my personal worship to a completely deeper place. I'm forever grateful.

Thank you, Pastor S. L. Walters. You taught me a lot!

Thank you, Dr. Sherby Clarke, for ordaining me into another level of ministry.

Thank you Bishop Carlton T. Brown for welcoming us and allowing us to grow in the ministry of the church.

The next seven devotional thoughts are based
upon the account found in
Luke 7:36-50.

All Biblical references are from the Authorized
King James Version (KJV)

WHAT'S INSIDE...

Introduction

In the beginning of the year 2002, in a small auditorium in downtown Brooklyn, GOD began something in the hearts of some youth and young adults who had assembled for a week of revival meetings. It seemed as if the whole event just came out of nowhere; but out of a simple suggestion came a week of singing, seeking, and sermons that would change the way we looked at worship—our worship, in particular.

While some did not and would not understand what was happening, there were those of us who knew there was something more to our Christian experience that we did not have, yet so desperately needed. Since that time, our hunger for GOD's presence and for His Word has not been satisfied; if anything, that hunger has intensified.

We still find ourselves desperately reaching out for more and discovering our reach has touched both friends and opponents. But like Mary, and like the unnamed "sinner woman", though we stumble, those of us who seek true worship will not be deterred until we touch not only the feet of Jesus, but the very heart of GOD! The fragrance we smelled that week was so unforgettable, that no other perfume will do.

This 7-day devotional is based on the incident at Simon the leper's house but it also draws upon elements from the anointing of Christ in Bethany by Mary, the sister of Lazarus and Martha. Powerful lessons on worship and instruction for the church are taught in these incidents which are similar but appear to be separate.

I invite you, therefore, to read our central text found in Luke 7:36-50 and the record of Jesus and Mary's encounter found in Matthew 26:6-13; Mark 14:3-9 and John 12:1-11.

Then join me as together we once again enjoy *The Fragrance of Worship...*

DAY 1

THE ALL-PURPOSE GOD

I Corinthians 15:27- For He hath put all things under His feet...

There is a mindset still prevalent, even among the children of God, which holds that some issues in our lives are beyond God's reach or outside of His interest. However, the Scripture is replete with references to the completeness of divine involvement in our lives:

II Chronicles 16:9–The eyes of the Lord run... throughout the <u>whole</u> earth...

John 1:3–<u>All</u> things were made by Him...

Ephesians 3:20 – [He] is able to do exceeding abundantly above <u>all</u> that we ask or think...

Philippians 4:13–I can do <u>all</u> things though Christ...

Like a king-sized blanket on a twin bed, God's coverage of human affairs is complete. No issue escapes His attention; no problem outwits His wisdom; no sparrow falls without His notice. He knows everything, He sees everything and He can do anything—He's an All-Purpose God!

The unnamed woman of Luke 7 must have understood this truth. Why else would she risk ridicule, rejection and maybe even death to worship Jesus at Simon's house? She must have known that the Lord could handle any detractor, forgive any of her sins and rescue her from the depths of her destructive lifestyle—at any level. So, she carefully planned her 'worship service', endured the whispers and the angry stares and found herself at the feet of Jesus. She worshipped at the feet of the One who not only knew her past, but held her future. She understood this and gave Jesus more than her gift—she gave Him *herself*. Jesus was truly her Lord; her King! She made a surrender that was as costly as that expensive alabaster jar of perfume. To the One who can do everything, she gave everything.

My friend, in order to have her breakthrough, you must make her sacrifice. Take that problem, that issue, that addiction, that talent, or that gift you have in your hands, and place it before the feet of the All Purpose God; and see if He won't do exceeding and abundantly above all that you can ask or think! And remember: you can't receive more than you presently have if your hands are already full!

Oh God, I've spent my whole life keeping certain areas out of Your reach. I want to change. I want to give You everything; I want to give You me! Please show me how...

DAY 2

FIND HIM

Matthew 11:28–Come unto me... and I will give you rest.

Should we take a moment to scan the landscape of our relationships, we would come up with at least one person who seems to be living life without direction, purpose or focus. Perhaps this person is in a persistent state of rebellion, confusion or even depression. And, very often, the people around this person resign themselves to dispensing the innocuous remedy contained in this statement:

"He/she needs to find him/herself."

I've got a better idea: *Find Jesus!* Are we all searching? Yes! Do we all need direction, purpose and focus? Yes! Do we need to live above the state of rebellion, confusion or depression? Most definitely! If this is the case and we recognize our situation needs changing, we've *already* found ourselves — and we don't like where we are! What we need is a sign post, a landmark, a guide, a spiritual GPS to get us out of where we are and take us where we need to be: We need to find Jesus!

This woman may have been a "nice girl" at one time — *but now she's a prostitute*. Once she heard about the MESSIAH, however, she knew her life had to change. So she went to Jesus: across town and out of the back streets where "appointments" were made; through the market place where her clients' wives might throw more than sharp glances and cold stares; past the temple where priests were waiting to stone her, *or to be with her*; past the doorway of Simon's house where disciples, weighed down with their own baggage, turned up their noses at her; all the way to the feet of Jesus where she found love, safety, forgiveness, and restoration.

Dear friend, go to Jesus; find Him! Do whatever you have to do: cover any distance, bypass any barrier, and circumvent any detractor in order to find Jesus. For only when we find the Master can we find love, hope, salvation, restoration... and ourselves!

Dear Lord, I've been looking for the right thing in the wrong places. I don't like where I am! I want to find You. You know where I am; lead me to a better place; reveal Yourself to me now, I pray...

DAY 3

THE REASON WHY...

—⚜—

*Isaiah 45:22–Look unto me and be ye saved...
for I am God and there is none else.*

Let's construct and conduct a quick survey.
Take the title of today's devotion, predicate it
with the following phrases and then complete
each sentence:

*The reason why I am a Christian...
a Churchgoer...*

You should have two (2) pretty clear-cut
responses to each sentence. If you're attending
a church and you don't know why, settle the
issue today! The vision that GOD has for you
should line up with the vision of the house
of worship you attend. Too many Christians

are out of the will of Christ; you don't have to be one of them! Whatever your reasons for going to church may be, however, know this: *Human beings were created to worship.* Going to church, therefore, should serve the supreme purpose of drawing us into an environment of worship. As a matter of fact, everything to which we devote our time, energy and resources that lies outside of the will of GOD, is really perverted worship. Hobbies, entertainment or vacationing are fine as long as GOD always has the first crack at our hearts, lives, time, and finances. Adam and Eve would not have fallen if they had trusted their God-given right to worship YAWEH rather than their own potential.

My point is that it is not enough to attend a church, to be part of a denomination or even to consider oneself a Christian. *We must be born again* (John 3:3); and like any other newborn we are completely dependent upon our Parent: JEHOVAH GOD. We feed off of Him through *worship* (See John 4:23, 24).

You and I have the responsibility to give GOD personal worship; not just to assemble with the congregation or to agree with the policies. Mary's worship wasn't a corporate activity — *it was a personal experience!* From our individual hearts we give GOD honor, reverence, adoration, love, and awe! When we bring these spiritual sacrifices and ourselves to Him, He can then bless us, enlighten us, and give us answers. Our hobbies, our possessions or our money can't do any of this. Only GOD — the Maker of Heaven and Earth — can give us the reason why...

Dear God, I am so used to following the crowd when it comes to You. I stand when they stand, sing when they sing, sit when they sit... but I want more, I need more. Free me to worship You personally, with my whole heart...

DAY 4

THE NEW MILLENNIUM SACRIFICE

Hebrews 13:15–By Him therefore let us offer the sacrifice of praise to God continually, that is, the fruit of our lips giving thanks to His name.

What a mess! Live animals: *everywhere*. Evidence that a live animal is in the building: *everywhere* (LOL)! Dead animals are there too. Throats cut; blood in bowls, blood on the furniture, on the priests' hands and on the hands of the parishioners. Such was the state of Old Testament worship. What a bother, what a hassle! So emotional, so expensive; thank God we don't have to do that anymore... do we?

For many of us the blessings of the New Covenant have been taken for granted, making worship cosmetic, antiseptic, well-rehearsed and clean, but not heartfelt. Many must have wept as they looked into the eyes of innocent lambs or doves moments before the blade of a knife ended their existence. And what about the *cost*: it was *always* the best lamb, the strongest goat, the perfect turtledove. But we say, "Ah, Jesus did away with all that! All the responsibility is on Him now! I can walk in and out of His presence and the most it may cost me is a couple of bucks..." Whoa! Is that what *real* worship is all about?!?

Friends, even today, true worship — worship that touches the heart of God, *real worship* — will cost something. Why doesn't GOD move like He did in Bible times? Because we don't worship Him like they did in Bible times. But when we bring Him our open hearts and minds; when we trust Him with our cares and burdens; when we study and live by His Word; when we give our best gifts; when we submit to His authority; when we pray in faith; when we abandon our pride, our self-consciousness and sometimes our decorum (see Mary and the unnamed sinner woman), GOD responds according to His good pleasure!

Mary and the sinner woman offered Jesus their best out of that alabaster box and everyone knew it was their best! They did it passionately with no concern for the opinions of the religious aristocracy. And today, if we expect to receive their breakthrough, then we must be willing to make their sacrifice. The question is, are you ready to make that kind of investment? Consider this: What will this praise cost you? If you sing that song, will it break your bank? If you lift your hands, will you over- extend your emotional budget? If you sing louder, will you cancel your pride payment? Are you willing to sacrifice your pride, your reputation, your "alabaster box"...for the sake of blessing Jesus?

Oh Jesus, how did Mary and that woman do it? Everyone is watching! Everyone knows me, everyone knows my past... how can I worship You passionately with everyone watching? Please Lord, reveal Yourself to me so strongly that all I see, all I care about, and all that matters is You...

DAY 5

THE TRUTH ABOUT YOUR CHURCH

John 8:32–Ye shall know the truth and the truth shall make you free.

The Church is the one agency that is responsible for representing the Kingdom of GOD on Earth, not the nation, nor the government, not even the individual. This singular responsibility falls upon the shoulders of the church. It is, therefore, a gravely serious matter when someone rejects Jesus because the church misrepresents the King or His Kingdom.

Some of us are blessed to be in churches with wonderful programs, fantastic music and state-of-the-art facilities. Others are favored to be involved in churches that have a tradition of service and evangelism to the community. I REPEAT: It is a blessing to be involved in such a ministry. But we must never forget that the church's primary duty is to rightly represent Jesus Christ.

All of our music, programs, and efforts must be for His glory. And while we should render service worthy of commendation, all praise must be returned to GOD, our Father, and the Lord Jesus Christ. "Let's have church" is an innocent yet unfortunate phrase; *worship is for Him, not for us!*

So what's the problem? The problem is that there are some in the church who serve GOD and others who serve themselves. Look at the stories of Mary and the sinner woman at Simon's house. They present a picture of the modern day church. In both instances house was filled, as are many church buildings, but the agendas of the congregants were as varied as a chameleon's appearance. Some came to see Jesus (praise GOD!), but others came to gawk at Lazarus. Some came to socialize, some came to work; some came to establish political alliances, some came to check Jesus out without ever intending to follow Him... and one came to plan betrayal. In each account, however, there was one who came to *worship*. And her worship changed the atmosphere as its fragrance filled the house. All eyes, some reluctantly so, were drawn to her while Jesus, and Heaven, picked her out of a crowded house by immortalizing her story.

Now ask yourself this honest question: When Heaven looks down upon *your* church and scans the congregation, does *your* worship stand out before GOD? Would Heaven pick you out of a crowded house of worship because of your passionate worship and devotion to GOD? Or are you among the countless others, mindlessly gathered to do everything else...except worship Jesus?

Oh GOD, I've gotten caught up... caught up in the meetings, music and the mundane traditions of church life. Begin a new season in me, open my eyes, and renew my mind by the power of the Holy Spirit. I don't want mere religion; I want a real relationship...let me see You and You only...

DAY 6

WHY ALL THE FUSS?

Isaiah 53:5-... *He was wounded for our trans-gressions... bruised for our iniquities... and with His stripes we are healed.*

What's the big deal? Why all the fuss?

Here's why: a lot of fuss was made on our behalf to get us out of the eternal mess we'd fallen into. GOD the Father, GOD the Son, GOD the Holy Spirit and the angels of Heaven have gone through a lot to save our drowning race. Gratitude, if not common courtesy, demands some sort of near-to-equal response, one would think. Alas, all of us do not feel that way.

It was Judas, the ministry treasurer at the "church gathering" in the Scriptures, who had the unmitigated gall to ask this question, "Why all the fuss?" It was a question that revealed the condition of his heart and his true feelings about the Lord: Jesus wasn't worth the trouble. Simon, himself a leper and the host of the "church gatherings", was equally brazen — questioning the calling and anointing of the Christ, the Son of the living GOD. In his eyes too, Jesus wasn't worth it.

But Jesus, knowing that He was soon to fulfill the prophecy given to Isaiah some 700 years prior, was about to show these men what He truly thought about the "sinner" turned worshipper. He turns to Simon and points out all of his shortcomings as a host: "Simon, You gave me no water for my feet (a common courtesy in those days) but this woman washed my feet with her tears. You gave me no kiss, but she hasn't stopped kissing my feet since I came in here (worshippers want intimacy with God)! You gave me no oil for my head, but she anointed my feet! She gave me full access to everything; even her most prized possession.

She anointed me in preparation for my Divine Assignment. In the other passages, Jesus prophesied that wherever the gospel was told, Mary's story would also be told; perhaps a last warning to Judas who would be remembered only for one horrible, but not unforgivable, act.

Today, Mary and that unnamed woman have been 'immortalized'; Judas has become infamous; Simon has been all but forgotten. It seems like a little fuss can go a long way!

So, what does this mean for you and me…?

Dear Jesus, the next time I meet You in church or in my quiet time, I want You to be blessed; I want You to feel welcomed, honored and loved. For what You've done for me, You are worthy of the best I can give You…

DAY 7

DON'T STOP

Philippians 3:13 & 14– ... forgetting those things which are behind, and reaching forth unto those things which are before, I press toward the mark for the prize of the high calling of God in Christ Jesus.

So what is the point of all this? Isn't it enough to be called a Christian? Isn't it enough to belong to a church? Isn't it enough to give an offering, do an occasional good deed and love my family? Isn't it enough to read the texts, sing the songs, and want to go to Heaven? *Isn't that enough???*

Well, my friend, my honest answer is "No". Even though all these things are good and, for the most part, necessary aspects of the Christian walk, we must never have a "minimum requirement" attitude when it comes to the will of GOD. Our GOD didn't take a minimalist approach when it came down to saving us! He emptied Heaven of its resources: every angel, every gift; everything has been given to us (and *for* us) to assure our salvation. Every power in opposition to His Kingdom has been overthrown due to the bloody yet victorious battle that Heaven has won. But most importantly, GOD gave us His most priceless treasure: He gave us JESUS and I'm so glad He did! Why? Because in Jesus we have the right to enter into GOD's eternal presence where there is joy, life and worship!

So, emulate the courage of our unnamed heroine or take a page out of Mary's book. Don't settle for a life beneath your privilege! Don't ever give up on yourself; don't ever give in to the enemy's pressure; don't ever give in to human detractors and naysayers; and please don't ever give up on GOD! He's there, He's near, He's reachable, He's accessible, and if you pursue Him passionately, He will reveal how passionately He feels about you! He'll embrace you and lift you to another level, high above the place you now occupy! If you turn to the Lord, you'll find Him waiting with His arms and His heart ready to receive you.

The Word says that He's not far from us and that the time to seek Him is now, while He can still be found (See Acts 17:27; Isaiah 55:6). The Bible also tells us that Christ *is* King! He's seated at GOD's right hand and through faith we are seated with Him right now (See Ephesians 2:4-7). What an awesome opportunity, with eternal consequences! Through spirit-and-truth worship, we can live in the atmosphere of Heaven right now! And in that atmosphere, the will of the King is always done!

So keep pushing, keep praising, keep pulling, keep pressing, keep praying, keep digging, keep worshipping, and whatever you do... DON'T STOP!!!

A PRAYER FOR YOU:

A s you consider what you've read this week I pray that the worshipper buried under years of pride, self-consciousness, or ignorance would rise up and come out. I pray that your passion for The LORD would reach new levels, even as you discover how passionate He is about you!

And finally, I pray:

"Oh LORD GOD, touch this dear person, who is reading these words, by the power of Your Holy Spirit. Help them to yield their praise, worship, devotion — their very lives to You. Save them if they don't know you personally. Impact their church, their families and their friends through their new level of intimacy with You. Adjust the atmosphere of their life so that it matches

the atmosphere of Your throne room. And, most of all, Father, fill their spiritual house with the Fragrance of Worship... in Jesus' name I pray, AMEN!

CPSIA information can be obtained
at www.ICGtesting.com
Printed in the USA
BVHW08s1232060818
523682BV00023B/1280/P